Six Ways To Enjoy This Strategic Coach Book

Text **60 Minutes**	The length of our small books is based on the time in the air of a flight between Toronto and Chicago. Start reading as you take off and finish the book by the time you land. Just the right length for the 21st-century reader.
Cartoons **30 Minutes**	You can also gain a complete overview of the ideas in this book by looking at the cartoons and reading the captions. We find the cartoons have made our Strategic Coach concepts accessible to readers as young as eight years old.
Audio **120 Minutes**	The audio recording that accompanies this book is not just a recitation of the printed words but an in-depth commentary that expands each chapter's mindset into new dimensions. Download the audio at **strategiccoach.com/go/Zoomingtoolkitebook**
Video **30 Minutes**	Our video interviews about the concepts in the book deepen your understanding of the mindsets. If you combine text, cartoons, audio, and video, your understanding of the ideas will be 10x greater than you would gain from reading only. Watch the videos at **strategiccoach.com/go/Zoomingtoolkitebook**
Scorecard **10 Minutes**	Score your Zooming Ahead Mindset at **strategiccoach.com/go/Zoomingtoolkitebook**. First, score yourself on where you are now, and then fill in where you want to be a year from now.
ebook **1 Minute**	After absorbing the fundamental ideas of the Zooming Ahead concept, you can quickly and easily share them by sending the ebook version to as many other individuals as you desire. Direct them to **strategiccoach.com/go/Zoomingtoolkitebook**

Thanks to the Creative Team:

Adam Morrison	Suvi Siu
Kerri Morrison	Christine Nishino
Hamish MacDonald	Willard Bond
Shannon Waller	Peggy Lam
Jennifer Bhatthal	Alex Varley

Zooming Ahead

When the COVID-19 pandemic hit, it was clear that it would impact all of our lives in important ways and we would have to drastically change the way we communicated with one another and did business. Would we fight back against the changes and wait for the "old normal" to return, or adopt new technologies and adapt to the new way of doing things? Though the Zoom video conferencing platform was already being used by individuals and businesses around the world, the pandemic made its use a necessity, and those who embraced it and mastered it thrived while those who resisted it would find themselves struggling to keep up.

When it comes to adapting to new circumstances, the question is, are you Zooming Ahead or being left behind?

Cartoons by Hamish MacDonald.

Printed in Toronto, Canada. The Strategic Coach Inc., 33 Fraser Avenue, Suite 201, Toronto, Ontario, M6K 3J9.

This publication is meant to strengthen your common sense, not to substitute for it. It is also not a substitute for the advice of your doctor, lawyer, accountant, or any of your advisors, personal or professional.

If you would like further information about The Strategic Coach® Program or other Strategic Coach® services and products, please telephone 416.531.7399 or 1.800.387.3206.

Contents

Introduction   6
Suddenly Bigger And Better

Chapter 1   12
Transportation Without Travel

Chapter 2   18
You're Here, You're There

Chapter 3   24
Suddenly 50x Bigger Future

Chapter 4   30
Ambition, Creativity, Cooperation

Chapter 5   36
Left Out, Left Behind

Chapter 6   42
Bypassing Bureaucracy

Chapter 7   48
Global Free Zone

Chapter 8   54
Is Zooming Ahead Fair?

Conclusion   60
Collaborative Individualism

The Strategic Coach Program   66
For Ambitious, Collaborative Entrepreneurs

Introduction
Suddenly Bigger And Better

You're amazed by the extraordinary new technological breakthrough that has transformed your vision of your personal and collaborative future.

Virtual conferencing technology existed before March 2020, but the global outbreak of COVID-19 and the subsequent lockdown made it a necessity for millions of people around the world to do business, hold meetings, and keep in touch with family and friends.

And the virtual conferencing platform that the majority of people turned to was Zoom.

Before the global lockdown, not enough people were using Zoom for it to reach its full potential. But suddenly it became a primary means of maintaining communication and teamwork, and we discovered that it's a medium that encourages ambitious, creative, and cooperative people to take advantage of one another's capabilities and creativity.

You've certainly had sudden jumps of opportunity and capability in the past, but it's likely that nothing can compare to what's happened to you, and, very importantly, to millions of others, during 2020 and 2021 with the worldwide adoption of Zoom. In the years ahead, when you look back with a greater sense of perspective, you'll probably see this "Zooming Ahead" year as the most remarkable turning point of your life.

Escaping from travel trap.

You've lived most of your personal and work life in a difficult and tiresome trap—the trap of having to travel in order to achieve important tasks and goals.

That's the way it had always been for humans. You had to travel to find food, to find other people, and to find shelter.

Travel time was ingrained in all of our calculations of what we could accomplish, and it was only when our ability to travel was taken away that we were motivated to find another way to transport ourselves for creative and cooperative purposes.

That's the amazing thing: this breakthrough wouldn't have happened if not for the pandemic. All these conditions had to be in place for humans to stop what they'd always been doing and start doing something different.

Now that you have the ability to Zoom Ahead, transporting yourself instantly with just a few mouse clicks, everything is liberating and lighter.

No more wasted normal.

Traveling was a waste of energy, a waste of time, a waste of money, and a waste of effort, but it's what we all had to do if we wanted to progress as individuals and groups.

We didn't realize how heavy the cost was and what an enormous waste it was until we were relieved of having to go through all of that time and effort.

When you think of the countless hours we used to spend just getting somewhere, it now seems incredible that we ever considered that normal. Now, since Zooming Ahead has become instantly and effortlessly available to us, the travel burdens we used to put up with seem absurd. All of that waste is now gone, and we don't want to bring it back.

In the days before the Zoom breakthrough, many of us traveled frequently because it was normal and we didn't want to get left out or left behind. But now that there's an alternative, we'll have options once travel is permitted again, and our conception of what's actually worth traveling for will change.

Everybody's sudden shift.

You've experienced a huge breakthrough because hundreds of millions of other ambitious and creative achievers like you are participating in the same global shift. In just the past year, the number of daily "Zoomers" has increased by 50x. And everybody taking advantage of Zoom is benefiting from everyone else.

This is the big thing about the digital world: progress is measured not by addition, but rather exponentially.

The technology wasn't as valuable when fewer people were using it and, therefore, fewer individuals to connect with. It went from 10 million connected users before the pandemic to 500 million users as the pandemic stretched on during 2020 and currently at the beginning of 2021. That increase is so great that it's difficult to even grasp how much opportunity has been delivered to the people who are skillful at using Zoom.

Indeed, this shift is unprecedented. We've never seen such an increase in such a short amount of time in terms of opportunity, capability, and payoffs for people who have a particular mindset based on ambition, creativity, and cooperation.

Ambition, creativity, cooperation.

You've become remarkably more ambitious over the past year, and more creative in ways that are markedly more cooperative with others. And you're doing all of this with other individuals who are much farther away geographically, some of them halfway around the world.

For Zoom to work, you have to be personally ambitious, and you have to be creative in ways that involve cooperation with other ambitious and creative people. Zoom doesn't favor anyone who is deficient in any of these three qualities, and people who lack ambition, creativity, and cooperation won't even recognize the purpose and advantage of Zoom in the first place.

Fresh start, new future.

All of this is something to stop and reflect on. It's as though you're getting a new start and a new future. Because of this extraordinary upgrade to your vision of what you can strive for and accomplish—totally different from your recent past—you now realize that your life before Zoom was all preparation for what's next.

Meanwhile, there are other people who are filled with resentment that the old ways of doing things have been interrupted. They want to go back to the old "normal." And they're going to be left behind.

But you're Zooming Ahead by recognizing that you can now achieve enormously bigger and better results than you ever could before with far less cost and effort and by taking advantage of this enormous opportunity for growth and change.

Chapter 1
Transportation Without Travel
You recognize that the crucial advantage of virtual conferencing is that you can go anywhere in the world without traveling.

If you experimented with virtual meetings before the 2020 global pandemic forced many of us to work remotely, you probably found that there weren't enough people using it to make it particularly useful in your daily work and personal life.

At Strategic Coach, which has offices in three countries, we'd already had some experience with virtual conferencing. It was certainly faster, but because live events were a more familiar alternative, we never made it our main focus.

Then, suddenly, a single year transformed "Zooming" into a worldwide, everyday capability for the most productive and creative individuals and teams. This is an amazing breakthrough in every area of our lives.

Before this happened, you may have been wondering and worrying whether there was any way your life and work could become more enjoyable in the years ahead. Now, suddenly, almost magically, this new Zoom way of instantly collaborating with others has transformed all of our future prospects and possibilities.

Huge productivity jump.
After just a few weeks of switching to working virtually due to the lockdown, Zoom users were achieving greater

results in much less time. This has been a huge productivity jump for cooperation and teamwork.

To create my quarterly small books, including this one, I work with a cartoonist, Hamish MacDonald, who usually isn't in the same city as I am. Since we began using Zoom to collaborate, our teamwork has drastically improved. We can see multiple documents and drafts on the screen at the same time, and go through the process together. Previously, we were always pressed for time to get the cartoons finished, and now we can get one chapter's cartoons finalized in only three days, cutting down about 70 percent of the time it used to take.

Viewing high-resolution videos and watching high definition TVs, we've all become very accustomed to, and have learned to expect, high-level visuals. And Zoom is the only company that saw this as a central factor and put together an experience we're used to.

The visuals on Zoom are of such high quality that you feel as though you're there with the other person. And since you don't have to travel to be with that person, Zoom is actually superior to in-person communication.

Eliminating wasted time.
We had all become so accustomed to traveling for many of our most important work and personal engagements that we didn't realize how much wasted time and energy were involved in all of these comings and goings. Travel involves calculating many factors—especially when traveling internationally—and requires operating according to other people's schedules.

Now, most of this wasted time and energy is being permanently eliminated by "Zooming" to our meetings.

I'd often wonder if there would come a time when I no longer wanted to make business trips to other cities, and it had nothing to do with the coaching activities I'd do when I got there. The hours spent both traveling and recovering from trips could total half-days.

We didn't often think about things like this because there was no alternative. But the moment everything changed due to the pandemic, even though we had to hustle to change direction and keep things going, I noticed I was experiencing less tension. I was sleeping better and exercising more.

And for every event that I was going to do via Zoom, I had more time to think through what was going to happen than I did when I was tired from traveling.

Faster results, less effort.

A Strategic Coach client from Singapore recently joined our virtual workshop at 10 a.m. Toronto time, which was 11 p.m. his time. I asked him if it was going to be a strain, and he said no, that he just rearranged his day so he could take a nap and then would be able to get eight hours of sleep after the workshop.

This is compared to the 23 hours it would take him to attend his workshop in person, with a connecting flight each way and dealing with jet lag for the following three or four days.

If you think back to all the effort that used to be required for those time-consuming travel meetings, you'll see how much faster and easier your results are being achieved now that you're meeting virtually.

No hassle, hurries, or delays.

We accept some degree of lateness in the in-person world, giving other people leeway and accepting their excuses for being late—because sometimes we need to use those excuses ourselves.

But with Zoom, there are absolutely no travel-related reasons why you should be late. You aren't traveling anywhere to get to your engagement. All the reasons for being late, for being unprepared, and for not being engaged are complexities that exist in the in-person world, not the Zoom world.

When you and others instantly "transport" yourselves to your Zoom meetings, the previous travel-related uncertainties are now eliminated. Your worries about being delayed by travel systems are gone. You're relaxed about being on time.

Endless technological improvements.

I believe that none of the old travel systems and methods were ever going to improve. There was never going to be an end to traffic, delays, accidents, malfunctions, breakdowns, and other factors beyond our control.

But with Zoom, which operates in the virtual dimension, thousands of innovations are converging to continually multiply the usefulness of this new way of transporting yourself in the future.

The old technological systems had reached a plateau, and now we recognize that Zoom is here and making things better for all of us.

TRAVEL
PILE-UP AHEAD
ARE WE THERE YET?
BOX
BUS
RRRRR!
I'M HERE! I'M HERE!
OLD WAY
SORRY, NOT MY PROBLEM
OOF!
FLIGHT CANCELL
WE TAKE NO RESPONSIBILITY
DERRY AIR

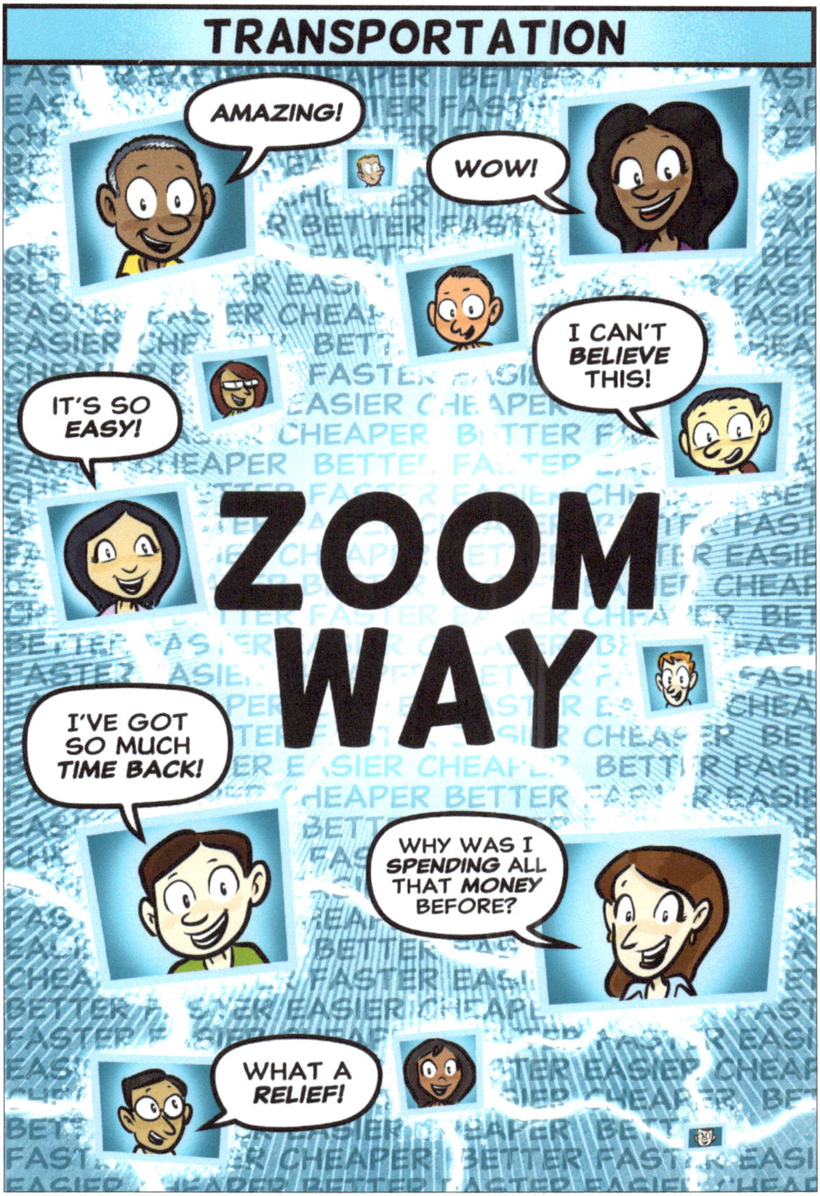
TRANSPORTATION
AMAZING!
WOW!
I CAN'T BELIEVE THIS!
IT'S SO EASY!
ZOOM WAY
I'VE GOT SO MUCH TIME BACK!
WHY WAS I SPENDING ALL THAT MONEY BEFORE?
WHAT A RELIEF!

Chapter 2
You're Here, You're There
You increasingly develop your Zoom capabilities so that for the rest of your work and personal life, you can both be where you are and collaborating somewhere else.

As you're becoming more Zoom capable and confident, you have a sense of being in a new lifetime.

Before Zoom became a personal capability for you and millions of other like-minded achievers, your most exciting sense of the future was strictly in your imagination, the stuff of daydreams that you couldn't put into action.

Now, with your new ability to be where you are and also virtually be somewhere else, you realize that you can take action right now on the things you want most in collaboration with other achievers who also imagine a bigger future.

Life before and after.
You can see your life so far as divided into two stages: getting ready for Zoom, and maximizing your Zoom capabilities after Zoom. Everything you've dreamed about and done up until now—your aspirations, efforts, and achievements—can now be multiplied in ways that previously weren't possible.

The people enthusiastically using Zoom are probably far more ambitious than those who have decided not to use it or are resisting using it. This means the Zoom community is a concentration of the most ambitious people on the planet.

The group of people using Zoom represents the highest level of ambition, creativity, and cooperation in the world, and it's gone from ten million users to half a billion users in a year.

The ambitious achievers using Zoom are conscious of this new capability, and when they log in to Zoom, they know that wasting people's time is not acceptable. Unlike what happens during in-person meetings (where the whole experience is often a waste of time!), when we use Zoom, we know that we have to be more intentional.

Transporting past obstacles.
Much of what you previously experienced as frustrations and failures were the predictable result of having to physically travel to get to meetings, conferences, and so on.

There are several components to this. First, there was the time you spent dreading having to travel. Second, there was the actual time and effort you put into traveling. Third, there was the fatigue you felt as a result of traveling and the regret over having had to travel. But you can now use Zoom to transform all of this past frustration into entirely new freedom.

Since Zoom is giving you back so much of your time, you now have the freedom to avoid booking meetings back to back to fit everything in. There's no longer any reason to get burned out by continuous meetings, and you also now have the time to prepare for and make the most of the time you're spending in meetings.

Expanding your collaboration.

In a single Zoom year, your experience of yourself as a mostly isolated and restricted striver has become a thing of the past. You can now confidently look forward to an achievement future where your biggest goals and best capabilities increasingly take the form of expanding collaboration.

Using Zoom, new things get created by people sharing their own vision, with others adding to it. And you can now meet with someone who lives next door and someone who lives halfway across the planet with the same degree of ease. You're no longer limited by geography.

Who you are is magnified by Zoom. If you don't like cooperating and collaborating, or being seen for who you truly are, then you won't like using Zoom. But that's an issue with your communication and your mindset, not with the Zoom platform.

Some people have been dragged kicking and screaming into this new Zoom way of doing things. Since you've *chosen* to use Zoom, you can feel capable and confident about your choice. This is the new normal, and one that will get better for the rest of your life.

Fresh intentions, fast result.

Sooner or later, with the old way of doing things, you might have run out of new ambition and achievements. Having to travel was likely becoming a growing force opposing your progress. Now, you're free to commit to the biggest goals of your life with the knowledge that everything is getting easier.

I can now come up with a new idea and immediately have a cooperative discussion around it, whereas before Zoom, a meeting would have to be scheduled for two weeks out, and plans, decisions, and teamwork would be delayed by the travel factor.

With the travel factor eliminated, you can now test out ideas in a 90-minute meeting that saves three months, at no cost. Your ambition is no longer constrained by circumstances. The limits are gone.

And now that you can instantly travel wherever you want, and meet with anyone you want, it changes what you think is important to talk about. Are you going to talk about ordinary things or something brand new? Zoom puts a sharp focus on what's valuable.

Multiplying the Four Freedoms.

The Zoom breakthrough has allowed us to expand our personal freedom in four key areas: time, money, relationship, and purpose. By not having to travel, the hundreds of entrepreneurs I spoke to over the first year of switching to operating virtually got about 30 percent of their time back. This extra time meant they could improve the quality and quantity of their relationships, and not having to travel meant they could transform the relationships they had with people they were separated from by geography.

Their money-making activity jumped, both due to the 30 percent bonus time they got back and their greater ability to work with the collaborative, innovative people they wanted to work with, unbound by geographical distance. They were also freed up to zero in on the things that were most important to them—their family, community, neighborhood, and causes—enhancing their freedom of purpose and bringing more balance to their lives.

ANYWHERE...
HERE
HERE
THERE
THERE
HERE
THERE
ERE
HERE
THERE
THERE
TH
HERE
THERE
HERE
THERE

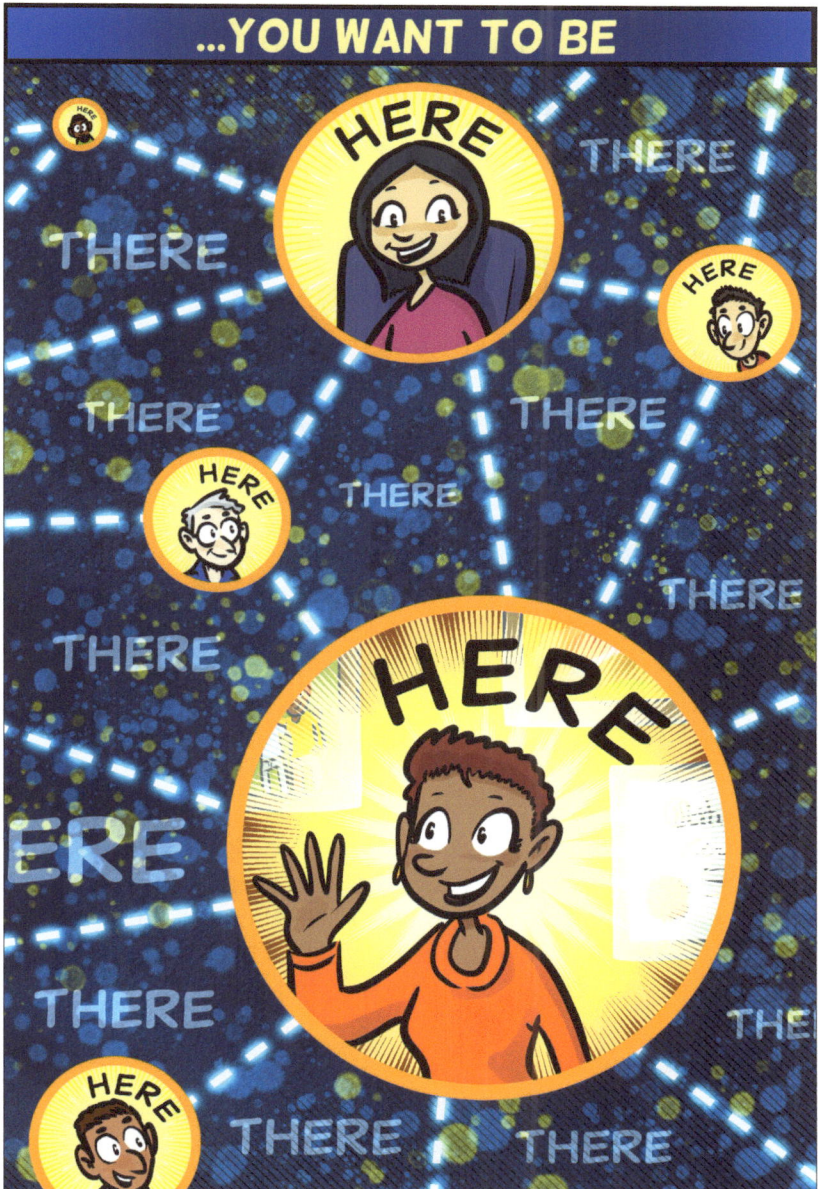

Chapter 3
Suddenly 50x Bigger Future
You realize that you can globally transport yourself because everyone you'll love to create and collaborate with in the future is now Zooming.

If you're the only person in the world with a telephone, then it's useless. If there are ten other people with telephones, then the value of your having a telephone is ten squared. And so on.

You may have accustomed yourself to using virtual conferencing some time ago and recognized the huge creativity and productivity gains that this technology offered. Then, in an amazingly short period of time, 50x more creative collaborators, all over the world, were now Zooming Ahead.

This is an amazing breakthrough for everyone who's in your future.

I've found that the people who are opposed to using Zoom tend to lack ambition, creativity, and cooperation. Because of this, they're getting left out and will continue to be left out as you and other achievers continue Zooming Ahead, creatively collaborating with one another.

Extraordinary breakthrough.
The massive growth of Zoom—50x in just a single year— is an extraordinary breakthrough for ambitious, forward-thinking individuals. Never before in human history had

so many of the most creative and collaborative people experienced such a huge new capability breakthrough.

The very nature of Zooming requires large numbers of people to be taking advantage of it. It's a networking capability, and so it has a networking effect. Metcalfe's law states that the economic value of a telecommunications network is equal to the number of connected users squared. Thus, the more users, the more valuable it is to each individual user.

Multipliers instantly available.

Due to the power of Zoom technology, your future results have been automatically multiplied. All around the world, there are new collaborators just waiting to meet you — without any travel required.

Everybody who can modify some aspect of what you're dreaming about, who can multiply what you're working on improving, and who can grow your teamwork is now available to you with just a few clicks on your computer or smartphone. You can collaborate, cooperate, and be creative with all of these people in a way that wasn't possible in the past.

These opportunities are brand new. In the past, we've always relied at least in part on traveling, even if it was just on foot. With Zoom, you're now going to be able to accomplish exponentially more than you ever were before by having access to all the right people for all the roles required to achieve the bigger and better future you envision.

New capabilities everywhere.

For most of your career, any capabilities that you wanted to add to your teamwork had to be available to you locally. Now, they can be located anywhere in the world.

Chapter 3

The nature of the Zoom breakthrough is that it's a shared experience. But each individual who is using Zoom is suddenly getting much better—expanding in ambition, creativity, and cooperation—and those improvements are happening "in secret" with the people they're expanding with.

There's no way for you to know about all the capabilities that are expanding via Zoom. It's that big a multiplier.

Your reach in finding new capabilities to collaborate with has gotten bigger, not by degrees, but rather exponentially, and you don't even have to think about it. All you have to do is take advantage of it. You can now get things done in a better, faster, easier, and cheaper way than you ever could before.

Not visible to "old" world.
Your Zoom breakthrough over the past year isn't apparent to most of the people in the world who are waiting for things to return to the "old normal."

Those people feel blindsided, disregarded, and attacked by the Zoom breakthrough because what they used to do is no longer considered useful.

Those who are taking advantage of the Zoom capability are keeping it quiet from those who aren't taking advantage of it as there's no point in sharing it except with other individuals who will take advantage of it and be useful to you.

If you aren't in alignment with the benefit of the capability, you won't even see the capability. People I know who are in bureaucratic situations are the ones who I've heard complaining about "Zoom fatigue." Meanwhile, the entrepreneurial clients that I speak to love it. And they're too busy being productive and enjoying this capability to try to convince those who are resisting it to use it.

True, but almost too good.

You may have daydreamed before about the kind of shift that's now happened, but that was just a daydream. Now, it's a totally positive reality every day, and it's almost too good to be true.

You may even wonder, "Can it really be this good all of a sudden?"

The answer is that it depends on whether you want it to be good. It will be as great as you want it to be. It will continually be better the more that you participate in it and the more that you create value doing it. It's exciting, but you have to contribute to the excitement.

Another question is whether you see the Zoom capability as being a temporary reality that's here until we can travel and meet in person again or a long-term reality that's here to stay.

Nothing in the physical world lasts forever, but Zoom is in the virtual world. And the people who would stop the capability aren't using it in the first place. They don't have the ability to stop it.

Those who are using Zoom won't want to suddenly give up easily multiplying their capabilities even once going back to the old normal is an option.

BIGGEST SUDDEN SHIFT...

Chapter 4
Ambition, Creativity, Cooperation
You are thrilled that it's your own ambition, creativity, and cooperation that motivate and enable you to increasingly Zoom Ahead with hundreds of others with the same qualities.

Whether you're able to appreciate the amazing Zooming Ahead opportunities before you depends on how much you had invested in yourself before this was possible.

The people who immediately took advantage of Zoom had already developed their ambition, creativity, and cooperation. They had over-prepared for the world they'd been living in and already done the exercise and muscle-building necessary to take full advantage of it. The new capability allowed them to become *more* ambitious, creative, and cooperative.

But for people who hadn't already worked on these qualities, Zoom didn't present much of a capability. Zoom is really only useful to the degree that you were prepared to take advantage of new technology before it became available.

Why you can Zoom.
You're able to use the sudden new capabilities of the Zoom technology to expand your impact and results *because* you already had the ambition, creativity, and cooperation to transform your growth and progress.

A lot of people think that technology creates transformations, but it's actually the other way around: transformations bring about technology. Unless there's a buildup of transformational aspirations on the part of a large number of people, the technology doesn't appear. Your and others' transformative power and aspirations brought about the great new capability of Zoom.

You were already in motion. You'd gained momentum in this direction of growth and weren't having anyone else do the heavy lifting for you.

You'd already taken responsibility for yourself and put yourself in a position where you could be rewarded with a brand new capability because of the investment you'd made in yourself.

You prepared yourself *before* asking for an opportunity, which is one of the key tenets of being an entrepreneur. You grew as best you could with the resources then available to you, so when something new happened, you were ready for it. But the something new only appeared as an opportunity because of your preparation.

Getting ready for this.
Now that Zooming Ahead is a new multiplier for you, it's totally transformed all your thinking about what you've achieved. All of your achievements thus far were preparation for what lies ahead. Zooming Ahead is your endless payoff.

Whatever existed for you before Zoom is multiplied with Zoom. Since you had focused on personal growth, and you prepared by working on your ambition, creativity, and cooperation, you're being rewarded for these strengthened qualities now that you're Zooming.

Zoom accelerates your growth and development. It's easier than it's ever been to find people with the capabilities you need to continue growing and achieving increasingly big results. It just takes a few clicks. There's no travel required.

Hard work suddenly easy.

You worked hard for your ambition, being creative required lonely courage, and cooperation came with many obstacles. But because you did all this on your own, all of it is now "Zoomingly" easy.

People who haven't strengthened their ambition, creativity, and cooperation are obstacles to you, not because they want you to fail, but because you have strengths they don't. People like this were unavoidable in the in-person world, but now, in the virtual world of Zoom, you don't have to interact with them.

You can avoid friction with people who don't have the qualities you have and are looking for in others, and restrict your Zoom meetings to only those people you want to be there. It's a bypass, taking you around the people who would hold you back from what you're aiming to do.

Millions of other achievers.

The individuals who are going to remarkably multiply your future have earned their way into the worldwide Zooming collaborative, the same way you have.

What this means is that you're benefiting not only from your own pre-Zoom preparation but also from everyone else's. Each of you now has access to each other's ambition, creativity, and cooperation.

This is the real Zoom payoff, and it's never happened before in human history.

You can be confident knowing that there are millions of people out there on Zoom and that they'll be responsive when you seek them out.

There was nothing like this in the pre-Zoom travel world.

Big investment, endless return.

Those who spent their pre-Zooming life investing in themselves, not expecting to be given a free ride, are now endlessly rewarded with all the exponential advantages of the biggest multiplier in history.

This is what you've been working for all along.

Some people say that technology has led to jumps like this before, but it's not true. No technology completely eliminated the need for traveling in order to link up with other people. Previous technologies have helped you improve as an individual, but they didn't create collaboration like Zoom is doing.

The telegraph, telephone, radio, and television were useful, and with the internet, there was the notion that there could be this collaborative breakthrough. Yet it didn't truly happen until the Zoom breakthrough.

Zoom isn't a broadcast medium. Best used, it's a collaboration medium. And those who are focused on collaboration will benefit most from it.

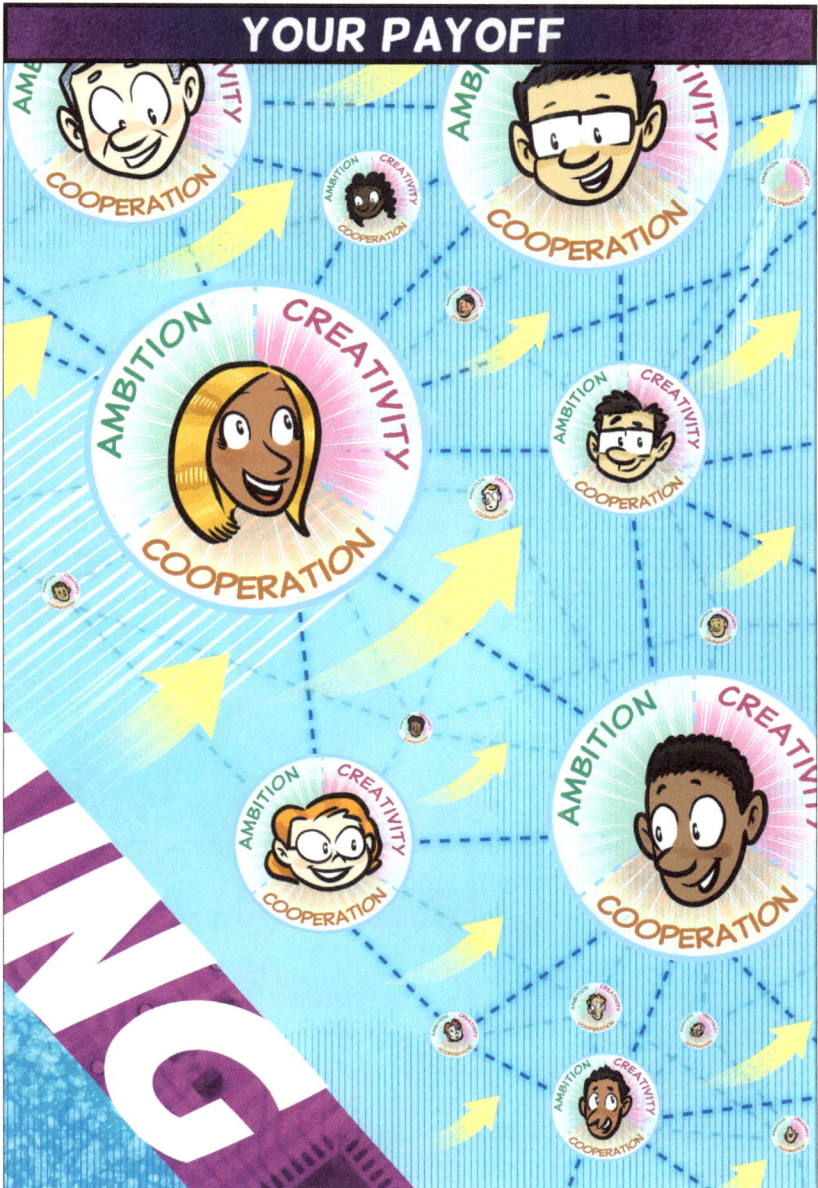

Chapter 5
Left Out, Left Behind

You notice more and more that individuals who aren't taking advantage of Zoom work and live in circumstances where they're not rewarded for ambition, creativity, and cooperation.

The people who are now becoming more Zoom-empowered were already in motion toward bigger capabilities and results before Zoom. Using Zoom simply accelerates where you were already going.

For people who work in bureaucracies, their most important ambitions, creativity, and cooperation can't take place inside their organization. This is because the whole purpose of a bureaucracy is to have a structure and process that isn't affected by individual ambition or creativity.

Those who don't take Zoom seriously also aren't serious about their own future because they can't express their future with great forward ambition, creativity, and cooperation. The only way they can progress is through continued promotion within a bureaucratic organization, which is limited by factors including seniority, time, and credentials.

Bureaucratic control of travel.
The huge differences between bureaucratic and entrepreneurial organizations might not have been as obvious before as they are now. Before, everyone had to travel, and a lot of the ways in which the bureaucratic world controls the entrepreneurial world are through the regulations and taxations that are imposed on travel.

You have to go through checkpoints, you have to have credentials and certifications, and these costly, limiting factors are all bureaucratic methods of controlling people who are outside of the bureaucracy.

Growing split everywhere.

There seem to be two separate worlds for working and living. One is the suddenly big Zoom world that keeps getting more useful and valuable for everyone who's taking advantage of its accessible capabilities, and the second is the old world where nobody understands how Zoom is changing everything and they're resistant to this change.

In the travel world, everyone was mixed in together, bureaucrats and entrepreneurs alike. All of us had to follow the same rules, and the travel world had become almost entirely bureaucratized. Now, we've gone from that to the Zoom world, which isn't bureaucratized. The only rules you have to follow are the rules of the technology.

Zooming—or not.

When you have a Zoom meeting on your schedule, it just takes a few clicks and you're where you want to be.

You didn't have to go through a great learning process to use Zoom. You already knew how to click. And there's no regulation or taxation to use it, only a service fee to use the highest level of the product, so you're actually paying for value.

People who lack ambition, creativity, and cooperation, and who aren't encouraged to strengthen those qualities, might use virtual conferencing, but they aren't getting the full benefit of Zooming.

They aren't using the technology to increase their ambition, creativity, and cooperation, and they aren't suddenly collaborating worldwide with people who are becoming more ambitious. All they're doing is dealing with the same issues they did before on a different platform.

The purpose of the technology is totally in favor of people wanting to be more ambitious. If you're in a bureaucratic organization and using Zoom, there seems to be a force that you're resisting. You get frustrated with the technology because it's asking you to do something that simply is not possible inside your circumstances—increasing your ambition, creativity, and cooperation. In a bureaucratic organization, you'll get punished for taking advantage of this technology.

Loss of "normal."

You probably know people who, before Zooming got big, seemed to be ambitious and resourceful in their work and personal lives, but since world events greatly disrupted the "normal" ways of getting things done, they've lost their sense of confidence and purpose.

Previously, there were all sorts of physical distinctions in the places where they worked that denoted superiority or inferiority—physical presence, attire, workstations, and even where people sat during meetings.

Then, everyone was told to stay home, which immediately eliminated all of those physical things that used to deter-mine status. In this sense, Zoom is disruptive to status and position. On a Zoom call, you can't tell who's at the head of the table. Indeed, Zoom disrupts interpersonal politics.

Feeling left out.

You can't provide a new breakthrough capability to individuals who are waiting for things to return to an old normal. You can sense they're aware that something new is happening all around them, but they don't understand what it is or why it's happening. They're not getting rewarded the same way they used to, and they're not getting rewarded in the new way either. So they're feeling left out.

For the most part, people who work in bureaucracies have been told since they were children what they should want. They get their goals from others, and their uniqueness has been drained out of them.

Zoom rewards those who think for themselves and who decide for themselves what they want. The Zoom capability is something these other people don't want, and you can't *want* someone else into wanting something for themselves. It has to be of their own initiative and volition.

Falling behind until waking up.

The Zoom breakthrough is uniquely individualized for everyone. You have to transform your mindsets before Zoom will multiply your capabilities, and those who don't want to transform themselves to take advantage of the opportunity will continually fall behind until they do.

Some people who have resisted so far will wake up and change their mindsets to take advantage of Zoom, but you can't predict who will because it's an individual choice, and you only fully know your own reasoning, not theirs. All you can do is choose to play a bigger, more exciting game with those who are choosing to play along with you.

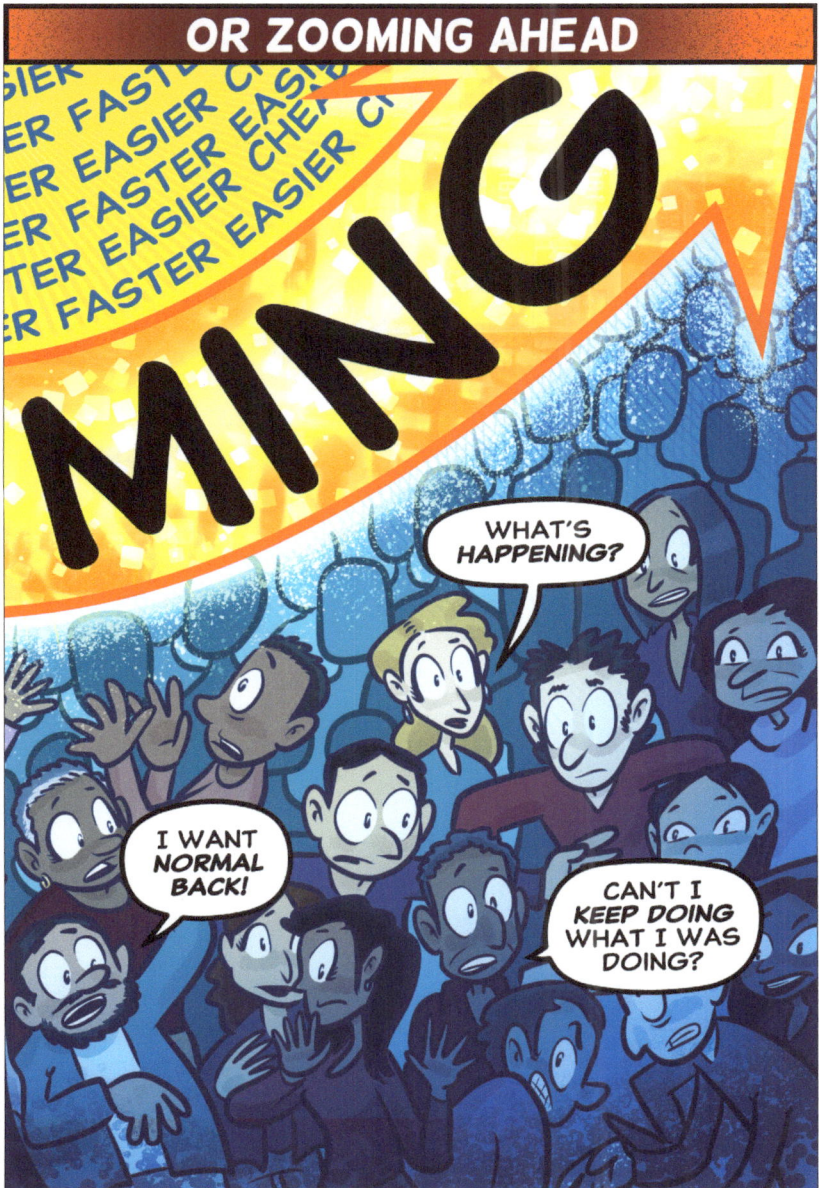

Chapter 6
Bypassing Bureaucracy
You're delighted to discover that for the foreseeable future, you can Zoom Ahead as fast and as fully as you want without bureaucratic interference.

For the next several years, maybe more than a decade, those who are mastering Zoom will have a bureaucracy-free opportunity to expand without a great deal of the regulation and taxation of the old way of getting things started in the travel-intensive world.

Just as happened with the introductions of newspapers, telegraphs, radio, television, and the internet, there's currently a burst of freedom with Zoom where individuals can do what they want to do.

Gradually, bureaucracy will want to control it, and lawyers and accountants will assert control over Zoom. But that will be sometime in the future.

Since bureaucrats haven't yet learned to Zoom Ahead, you can bypass them right now and make enormous progress.

Bureaucracy doesn't like it.
You've probably heard from people who work in corporate and government bureaucracies that doing work by virtual conferencing doesn't improve their work and personal lives.

That's because Zooming Ahead on the part of hundreds of millions of other individuals undermines all bureaucratic predictability. In the travel world, bureaucracies could much better monitor who was doing what and with whom. In the Zoom world, they can't know who's meeting with whom and about what.

Zoom has removed the complexities of the travel world, making life more predictable for ourselves—and far less predictable for bureaucracies.

The entire bureaucratic world is made up of people who have credentials but not necessarily capabilities. But Zoom rewards capabilities, not credentials. No matter what credentials you have or don't have, you can be effective using Zoom or not based solely on your capabilities.

Can't control others' futures.

Every bureaucratic organization exists to control the mindsets and behaviors of individuals outside of the organizations in such a way that no new innovations or collaborations will occur that unpredictably threaten their future existence.

Facebook, Twitter, and Google are all bureaucracies. And bureaucracies are scared of anyone coming up with a new idea that might threaten the bureaucracy's continued existence.

But the individuals who are Zooming Ahead are using the new capabilities to expand and grow their futures, using their ambition, creativity, and cooperation to move toward bigger and bigger goals. And bureaucracies can't stop this from happening.

There's nothing preventing people from using Zoom to create the futures that they want for themselves. Zoom isn't regulated in that way, and so ambitious individuals using it are free to fully use and further strengthen their ambition.

Sudden new solutions.

Within the first year since the pandemic necessitated a move to virtual conferencing, you've discovered and used Zooming Ahead opportunities to create uniquely new solutions that bureaucratic organizations can't see or prevent. The more you take advantage of this, the more solutions you'll create.

And the new solutions you create will exist beyond the notice of bureaucracies. This new normal won't last forever. We have a window of opportunity where we can Zoom Ahead almost without notice.

Zoom rewards those individuals who want to use it to enhance their ambition, creativity, and cooperation, and everyone else is just continuing to operate in a place of lonely competition. In other words, if you've prepared for this, you're now riding the wave, and if you haven't, you're going to feel left out, and things are going to be difficult and lonely for you.

Invisible new teamwork.

All of your creative new teamwork within your worldwide Zooming is increasingly more productive and valuable than any of the controlling structures and processes inside of any bureaucracy you encounter. Your expanding Zoom teamwork right now can't be seen or prevented by bureaucracy.

When I compare this year's experience to the previous 76 years of my life, this is by far my best year ever.
The removal of travel has made teamwork so much

easier, cheaper, faster, and more satisfying than it was before. People are no longer late, people are no longer unavailable, and you don't have to schedule far ahead in the future anymore to meet with the people you want to meet with.

This time period right now is a once-in-a-lifetime window for making great, extremely fast progress. It's special, and we need to appreciate it and take full advantage of it.

Available now, but not forever.
All bureaucracies in the world are going to attempt to regain the control they're losing during this sudden Zooming Ahead period. So, we're going to use this extraordinary opportunity to Zoom Ahead as quickly and fully as we can to enjoy our bureaucracy-free advantage.

It's an important skill to understand that something might be possible right now, but it won't be possible forever. You'll lose the opportunity if you take it for granted and wait to act on it.

And with Zoom, you don't have to "get ready to get ready." You've already prepared for this, so you can just do it. In the time we have while Zoom is free of bureaucracy, you can become more capable every single day that you take advantage of it.

You're already used to doing what you need to do to take advantage of Zoom because it simply involves continuing to be who you are and investing in yourself.

Chapter 7
Global Free Zone

You keep getting more evidence that your mastery of Zoom enables you to continually expand your global entrepreneurial success, virtually free of competition.

Here's a secret you may want to keep to yourself, and it's one that may have occurred to you already: none of your competitors know what you're doing with your expanding Zoom innovation and collaboration. They haven't got a clue about how you've been Zooming, about what you're doing now, or about what you're going to be doing in your Zooming Ahead future.

It's a "Free Zone," which is what we call an area of opportunity for value creation that hasn't yet been discovered or influenced by competitors.

And the Zoom technology is instantaneous, whether you're talking to someone in the same time zone as you or someone many time zones away. You can engage in projects, deals, and collaborations in a far broader geographical area, with a much greater scope of whom you can work with and whom you can have as clients.

Not like the old marketplace.
Everything you might have experienced and expected for your future has suddenly ended. None of the old rules of success apply to the Zooming Ahead opportunities and capabilities that are now available to you.

And everything you do while you're Zooming Ahead is 100 percent invisible to anyone who'd want to regulate it in any way. It's binary, with everyone either entirely seeing what's happening with Zoom—or not seeing it at all. And for bureaucracies, it's not at all.

There's nobody watching what you're creating, and there's nobody watching your transactions, except for the people you're choosing to get involved with.

There's nothing holding you back except old mindsets. And if you've spent enough time Zooming Ahead, you know that these new opportunities are real and that there's no reason you can't discard all the mindsets that applied only to the pre-Zoom world.

Your network is uniquely yours.

All progress you make in extending your Zooming Ahead networks of innovation and collaboration will always be your unique property. No one else knows about the connections you're making and developing. All of your progress and growth is uniquely your own.

A lot of the grievances and drama humans have experienced throughout history have related to physical space. Whether it's wars between countries or disputes between neighbors, it's about space and how two people can't occupy the same space at the same time.

But on Zoom, 500 million people *can* occupy the same space at the same time. Plus, you only have to interact with the people you've chosen to interact with, and you don't waste anyone's time who doesn't have to be in your meetings.

That last point is another example of things being binary, because someone's either important for a project or they're not. Zoom brings this into clear focus.

As global as you want it.

You may have been previously restricted to local success in your business. The laws of travel may have prevented you from aspiring or achieving further afield. But now, if you were local, you can expand to regional, regional can now expand to national, and national can now become global.

Each of us tests our reach one stage at a time, expanding further with each stage, but everyone who enthusiastically got involved in Zoom as soon as we were compelled to is now doing business much further afield than they were before. And that refers not only to having clients farther away, but outside collaborators and even team members too. Business owners are opening themselves up to the idea of working with team members they might never meet in person.

All future progress is "free."

You might only be getting the financial evidence now, but it will soon become clear to you that Zooming Ahead is permanently less costly than the old travel-intensive world.

Strategic Coach has always involved travel. Clients in Australia, for example, often book off four to five days to attend their one-day workshop in Toronto or Chicago. Now, they only need to account for the time difference because with a few clicks, anyone anywhere in the world can instantly be transported to their Strategic Coach workshop.

And this sudden new expansion of our capability and reach is coming at almost no cost for us or for our clients.

It would have cost us more to double our size in the travel world than it's costing us to go 10x in the Zoom world.

With Zoom, most of the travel costs are eliminated, of course, but something that's perhaps not yet as obvious is that far easier innovation and collaboration are almost free, as well.

Nothing's holding you back.

Those who are addicted to always having excuses for their lack of progress and success will never take advantage of the new Zooming Ahead advantages. Their mindsets are their obstacles.

Those who are afraid of Zoom are making things up to scare themselves, and their biggest fear is that they're not equal to the opportunity in front of them. They question whether they're good enough as entrepreneurs to have bigger ambitions and creative enough to take advantage of this new tool.

They had achieved success in the old world, but now they feel like they've reached the top of the ladder only to discover it had been leaning against the wrong wall. They're angry about the new changes, but they're the only ones standing in their way of becoming more successful in the Zoom world.

You, on the other hand, are Zooming Ahead as fast as you can because you know that you no longer need to worry about anyone holding you back.

A NEW DIMENSION

Chapter 8
Is Zooming Ahead Fair?
You investigate and decide that the great breakthroughs, advantages, and payoffs you're gaining from Zooming Ahead are totally fair.

You might be wondering whether it's fair that you're gaining an advantage through the use of Zoom, but the fact is that you haven't taken anything from anyone else to gain your success. No one is worse off because you are better off.

It all goes back to the investments you made in yourself before Zooming Ahead was possible. You expanded your ambition, you experimented to be more creative, and you cooperated with others—all when there was no guaranteed return for doing any of this.

The idea of fairness is inextricably tied to our concept of space: who gets to be where and who gets access. Now, everyone with a computer and internet connection has access to Zoom. And those who are using it to connect with others and achieve great breakthroughs aren't taking up space.

The people who have been resisting using Zoom could have also been using it this whole time. But they hadn't invested in their ambition, creativity, and cooperation like you had, so for them, Zoom didn't represent the same opportunity.

New opportunities don't care.
When new opportunities for your individual improvement are suddenly available, it's totally up to you to take advantage of them. There's no predetermined lineup of who

deserves to benefit either first or most from the new possibility. Opportunity doesn't care about anyone in particular.

Opportunities come about when certain factors are in place, and a whole new capability—and a whole new possibility—develops. It has nothing to do with fairness. It isn't a moral issue. If you're alert, curious, responsive, and resourceful, then something new becomes possible.

And if you don't check all of those boxes, then you won't even see the opportunity. You'll just see that some other people are happier, less stressed, and making more money.

New capabilities are unpredictable.

There's nothing in the past that automatically determines what new capabilities are going to suddenly multiply the existing capabilities of certain people, enabling them to jump ahead of many others. But you do know that being open to unpredictability is a useful mindset.

For entrepreneurs, it isn't uncommon for unpredictable things to happen. You obviously can't plan for something you can't predict, but you can be prepared for the fact that unpredictable things will occur. So, we make sure we're prepared for surprises because surprises are part of the entrepreneurial world, which is where we've chosen to live.

While other people suffer from having rigid mindsets, when something unpredictable occurs, the best entrepreneurs acknowledge what's no longer possible, but also what's now possible that wasn't before.

Breakthroughs reward preparation.

Zooming Ahead is an enormous reward for previous investments you made in yourself—not because you had the right credentials and belonged to the right group, and not because you were the same as everyone else, but because you were uniquely different.

It's training and preparation that allow you to be immediately useful in new circumstances. After all, you can't be the hero to an injured person in an emergency unless you know first aid.

I've personally gone through economic setbacks that I've learned from, and I've lived in societies and economies that have had economic setbacks, and I've learned from those. So, when all of a sudden in 2020 the very basis of our entire revenue—hosting workshops and coaching entrepreneurs—was taken away by a global event, we were prepared to take the time to figure out a new way of doing things.

The technology was already there, and it became extraordinarily more powerful when the other way of doing business was no longer an option.

Nothing new is needed.

Often, when a new technology is released, it's version 1.0 and there's an expectation that while you get used to it, the creators are going to constantly improve it in order to handle the things they're not handling right now and fix any bugs.

However, in one year of using Zoom, I haven't found anything lacking in the technology. In fact, in 25 years, if Zoom were exactly the way it is now, that would be perfectly fine with me.

I have a sense that the company must have done an enormous amount of preparation for this situation because of the way they multiplied so quickly when it became necessary and because of the way their service seems to be flawless. I've been amazed at the simplicity and satisfaction of the experience over the past year.

Better than normal.

Many people refuse to Zoom Ahead because it isn't "normal," which is to say it's not like the old predictable and comfortable way of getting things done and getting along.

When they say they want to go back to normal, what they're saying is that they're totally unprepared for anything better. What they call normal is simply what they've gotten used to.

But what's considered normal is an ever-changing thing. It's not static. What was normal for us ten years ago was very different from what was considered normal 50 years ago.

And for those of us who recognize that what's normal is constantly changing, Zooming Ahead has become our normal. Our circumstances changed, we quickly adapted and took advantage of a new way of doing business, and now Zooming Ahead is just what we do.

If someone tells me that they don't like using Zoom, I'm not going to get into the conversation with them. I don't think it's unfair that I'm 100 percent taking advantage of it while they're not, yet I also know there's nothing I can do to change their mindset. But when I meet other people who are Zooming Ahead in unique ways, we share our excitement with one another, knowing that things are getting bigger and better.

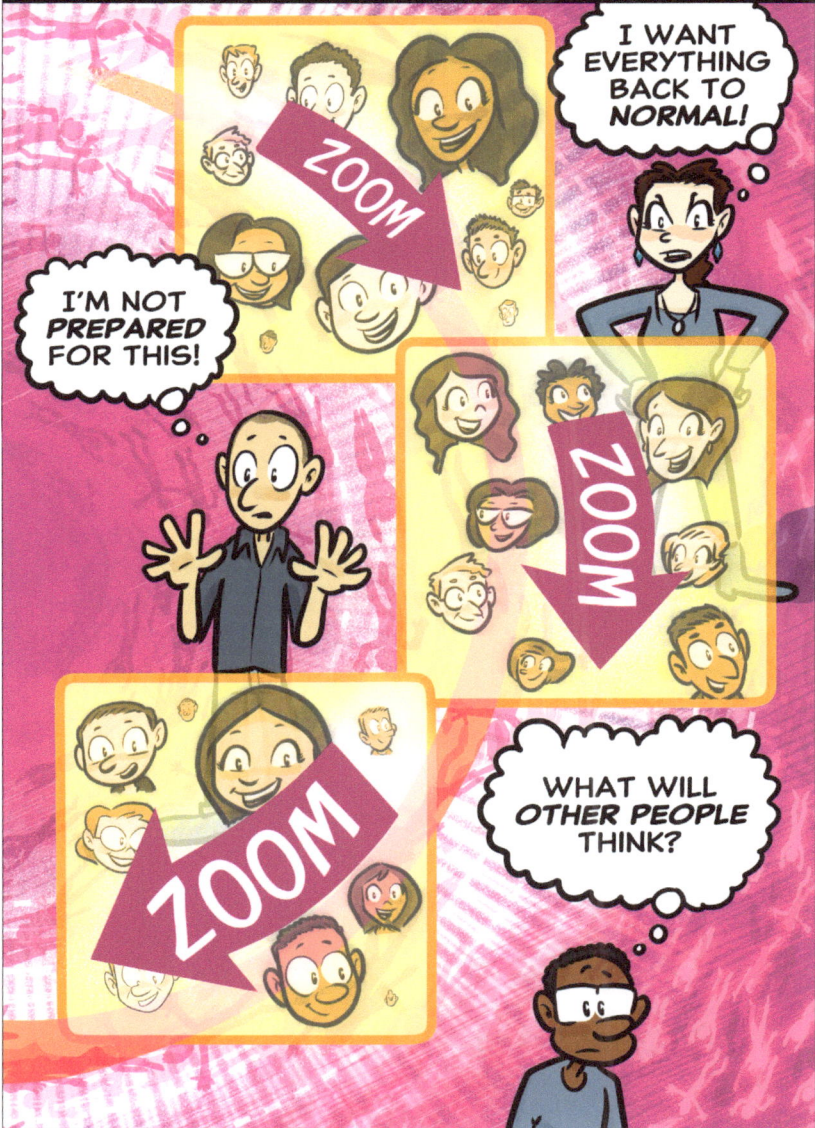

Conclusion
Collaborative Individualism
Your confidence about your personal future continually multiplies because Zooming enables you to innovatively profit from expanding worldwide cooperation.

The sudden technological opportunity that Zoom represents marks a dramatically new, better, and different way to succeed as an ambitious individual in comparison to what you imagined was possible perhaps just a year or two ago. Not everyone will take advantage of it, but Zooming Ahead is an opportunity that you are choosing for yourself.

There's a mindset requirement to take full advantage of Zoom. You have to have ambition, creativity, and a desire to grow exponentially through collaboration with others. If you don't, you can use Zoom, but you won't be getting the real payoff of the platform, which is the opportunity to multiply your capabilities by collaborating with other capable, ambitious people using Zoom all around the world.

If you bring your ambition, creativity, and cooperation to the table, Zoom will enhance all those qualities. If all you do is passively log on, you might as well be hiding from the opportunities.

Only individuals qualify.
This new Zooming Ahead realm of engagement and achievement is available only to those who choose to be individuals. You have to be committed to your own uniquely individual ambition, creativity, and cooperation

before Zoom can work for you. Entering on behalf of others doesn't work. You can only represent yourself.

Everyone who's experiencing the greatest success with Zooming Ahead put time and energy into getting ready for Zoom before they even knew about it. They worked on expanding those three qualities—ambition, creativity, and cooperation—in themselves before they were aware of what the enormous reward would be, and doing this is what made them ready to use Zoom to expand those qualities in far greater ways than they could have imagined.

On the other hand, people in bureaucratic organizations were totally unprepared to take advantage of Zoom's opportunities.

Bureaucracy not admitted.

Old industrial ways of collecting and controlling people within rigid structures and processes don't work inside of Zoom. All attempts to create superior/subordinate rankings and top-down conformity make no progress on Zoom, and people with bureaucratic agendas make no sense there.

On Zoom, you arrive as an equal member. There's no one sitting at the head of the table, and there are no other indicators of rank that we're used to from the bureaucratic world.

All bureaucratic distinctions, restrictions, and limitations have been completely left out of the program. This means that everything that makes bureaucracy meaningful is 100 percent absent from Zoom. And bureaucracy sticks out on Zoom because of the way the technology connects people.

People who attempt to get the benefits of Zoom that entrepreneurs are getting, but who also assert that the old, bureaucratic ways of doing things should be back in place, get shut down. The ambitious, creative, cooperative achievers who are Zooming Ahead are fully aware that this new way is better for everyone, so pushing for bureaucracy will mean that you get dropped from the call and replaced with an individual who has a cooperative attitude.

Only collaboration works.

You've always wanted to be collaborative, but before Zooming became available, it was often a difficult task, requiring long, lonely stretches of courage.

What's amazing about Zooming Ahead is that everybody's best collaborative instincts, mindsets, and capabilities are valued, rewarded, and multiplied.

There's still a place in the world for bureaucrats, but conformity isn't rewarded on Zoom. What's rewarded is your uniqueness as an individual. People care about what your unique capabilities are, and in order for you to use and grow those capabilities in collaboration with other individuals, it's a requirement that you have a cooperative mindset.

Growth is guaranteed.

All collaboration with other creative individuals inside of Zooming Ahead structures and processes automatically leads to everyone's growth. This growth triggers new ambition for everyone, and everyone's growing ambition generates new collaborative breakthroughs.

Each person in a collaboration contributes something unique, and each person in the collaboration gains the benefit of working in cooperation with one another. When working with like-minded collaborators, there are now no limitations due to status or location. And the time, money, and energy that were required when traveling are no longer limiting factors either. Entrepreneurs can collaborate and grow together without any of the burdens that used to be a necessary part of trying to achieve a bigger future.

Everyone who's doing this keeps getting better at using Zoom, which means there is less and less of a limit on the aspirations and ambitions they can pursue in using it.

Choosing to multiply futures.

Until Zooming Ahead became suddenly available, everyone was faced with the anxiety-inducing task of creating their own future. This invariably required being disconnected and in competition with others.

Individual self-development involved people vying for the same scarce rewards. As you reached higher platforms, fewer people could join you, making you feel lonelier and causing you to feel that you had to hide your success from others who saw you as using scarce resources for your own individual good.

Now, with Zooming Ahead, everyone's future growth multiplies the future growth of everyone else. The collaborative nature of Zooming Ahead has taken us from competition into collaboration, where no individual's advancement means another individual's lack, and where every individual making great headway inspires, encourages, and supports every other individual making great headway.

It isn't a zero-sum game or a win-lose game anymore. It's a plus game.

BEING YOURSELF...
ZOOMING
ZOOMING
ZOOMING
ZOOMING
ZOOMING
ZOOMING
ZOOMING
ZOOMING

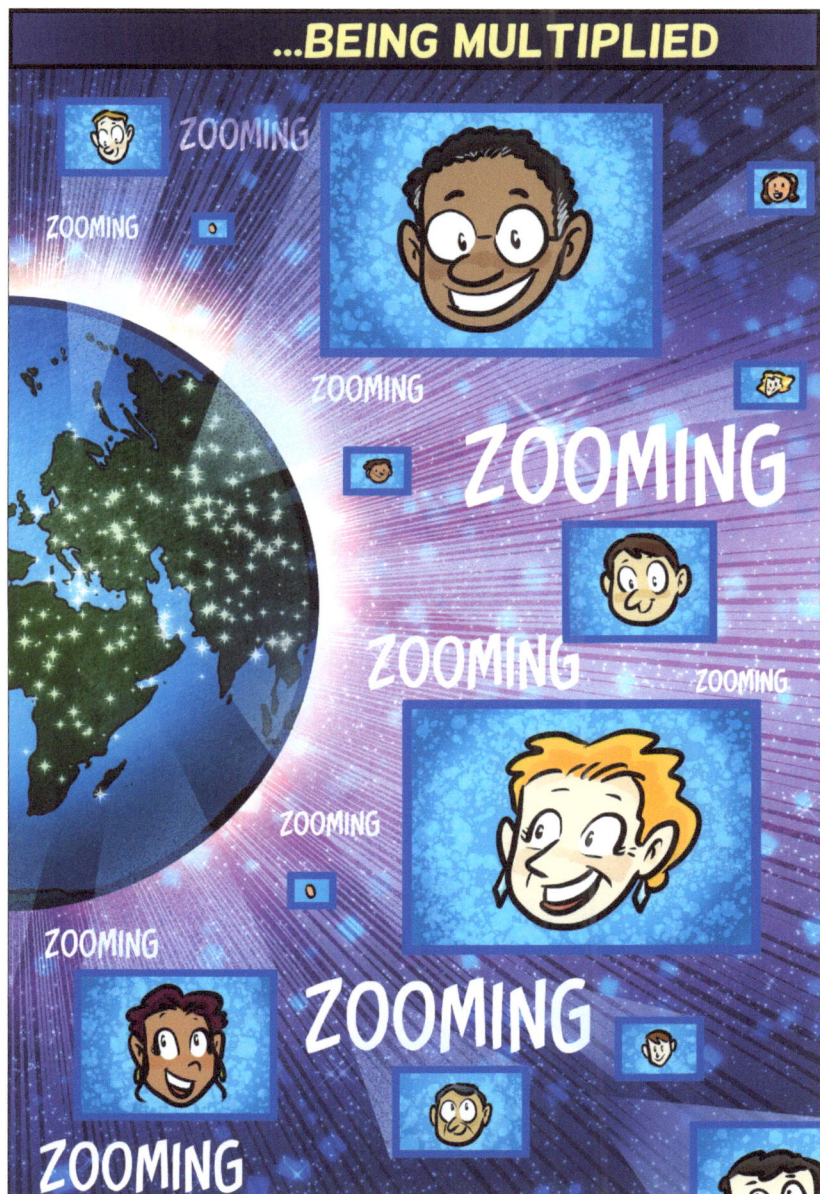

The Strategic Coach Program
For Ambitious, Collaborative Entrepreneurs
You commit to growing upward through three transformative levels, giving yourself 25 years to exponentially improve every aspect of your work and life.

"Zooming Ahead" is a crucial capability and a natural result of everything we coach in The Strategic Coach Program, a quarterly workshop experience for successful entrepreneurs who are committed and devoted to business and industry transformation for the long-term, for 25 years and beyond.

The Program has a destination for all participants—creating more and more of what we call "Free Zone Frontiers." This means taking advantage of your own unique capabilities, the unique capabilities around you, your unique opportunities, and your unique circumstances, and putting the emphasis on creating a life that is free of competition.

Most entrepreneurs grow up in a system where they think competition is the name of the game. The general way of looking at the world is that the natural state of affairs is competition, and collaboration is an anomaly.

Free Zone Frontier
The Free Zone Frontier is a whole new level of entrepreneurship that many people don't even know is possible. But once you start putting the framework in place, new

possibilities open up for you. You create zones that are purely about collaboration. You start recognizing that collaboration is the natural state, and competition is the anomaly. It makes you look at things totally differently.

Strategic Coach has continually created concepts and thinking tools that allow entrepreneurs to more and more see their future in terms of Free Zones that have no competition.

Three levels of entrepreneurial growth.

Strategic Coach participants continually transform how they think, make decisions, communicate, and take action based on their use of dozens of unique entrepreneurial mindsets we've developed. The Program has been refined through decades of entrepreneurial testing and is the most concentrated, massive discovery process in the world created solely for transformative entrepreneurs who want to create new Free Zones.

Over the years, we've observed that our clients' development happens in levels of mastery. And so, we've organized the Program into three levels of participation, each of which involves two different types of transformation:

The Signature Level. The first level is devoted to your *personal* transformation, which has to do with how you're spending your time as an entrepreneur as well as how you're taking advantage of your personal freedom outside of business that your entrepreneurial success affords you. Focusing on improving yourself on a personal level before you move on to making significant changes in other aspects of your life and business is key because you have to simplify before you can multiply.

The second aspect of the Signature Level is how you look at your *teamwork*. This means seeing that your future consists of teamwork with others whose unique capabilities complement your own, leading to bigger and better goals that constantly get achieved at a measurably higher rate.

The 10x Ambition Level. Once you feel confident about your own personal transformation and have access to ever-expanding teamwork, you can think much bigger in terms of your *company*. An idea that at one time would have seemed scary and even impossible—growing your business 10x—is no longer a wild dream but a result of the systematic expansion of the teamwork model you've established.

And because you're stable in the center, you won't get thrown off balance by exponential growth. Your life stays balanced and integrated even as things grow around you.

And that's when you're in a position to transform your relationship with your *market*. This is when your company has a huge impact on the marketplace that competitors can't even understand because they're not going through this transformative structure or thinking in terms of 25 years as you are. Thinking in terms of 25 years gives you an expansive sense of freedom and the ability to have big picture goals.

The Free Zone Frontier Level. Once you've mastered the first four areas of transformation, you're at the point where your company is self-managing and self-multiplying, which means that your time can now be totally freed up. At this stage, competitors become collaborators and it becomes all about your *industry*. You can consider everything you've created as a single capability you can now match up with another company's to create collaborations that go way beyond 10x.

And, finally, it becomes *global*. You immediately see that there are possibilities of going global—it's just a matter of combining your capabilities with those of others to create something exponentially bigger than you could ever have achieved on your own.

Global collaborative community.

Entrepreneurism can be a lonely activity. You have goals that the people you grew up with don't understand. Your family might not comprehend you at all and don't know why you keep wanting to expand, why you want to take new risks, why you want to jump to the next level. And so it becomes proportionately more important as you gain your own individual mastery that you're in a community of thousands of individuals who are on exactly the same journey.

In The Strategic Coach Program, you benefit from not only your own continual individual mastery but from the constant expansion of support from and collaboration with a growing global community of extraordinarily liberated entrepreneurs who will increasingly share with you their deep wisdom and creative breakthroughs as innovators in hundreds of different industries and markets.

If you've reached a jumping off point in your entrepreneurial career where you're beyond ready to multiply all of your capabilities and opportunities into a 10x more creative and productive formula that keeps getting simpler and more satisfying, we're ready for you.

For more information and to register for The Strategic Coach Program, call 416.531.7399 or 1.800.387.3206, or visit us online at *strategiccoach.com*.

THREE LEVELS OF
FREE ZONE FRONTIER

25	26	27	28
29	30	31	32
33	34	35	36

10X AMBITION

13	14	15	16
17	18	19	20
21	22	23	24

SIGNATURE

1	2	3	4
5	6	7	8
9	10	11	12

FREE ZONE

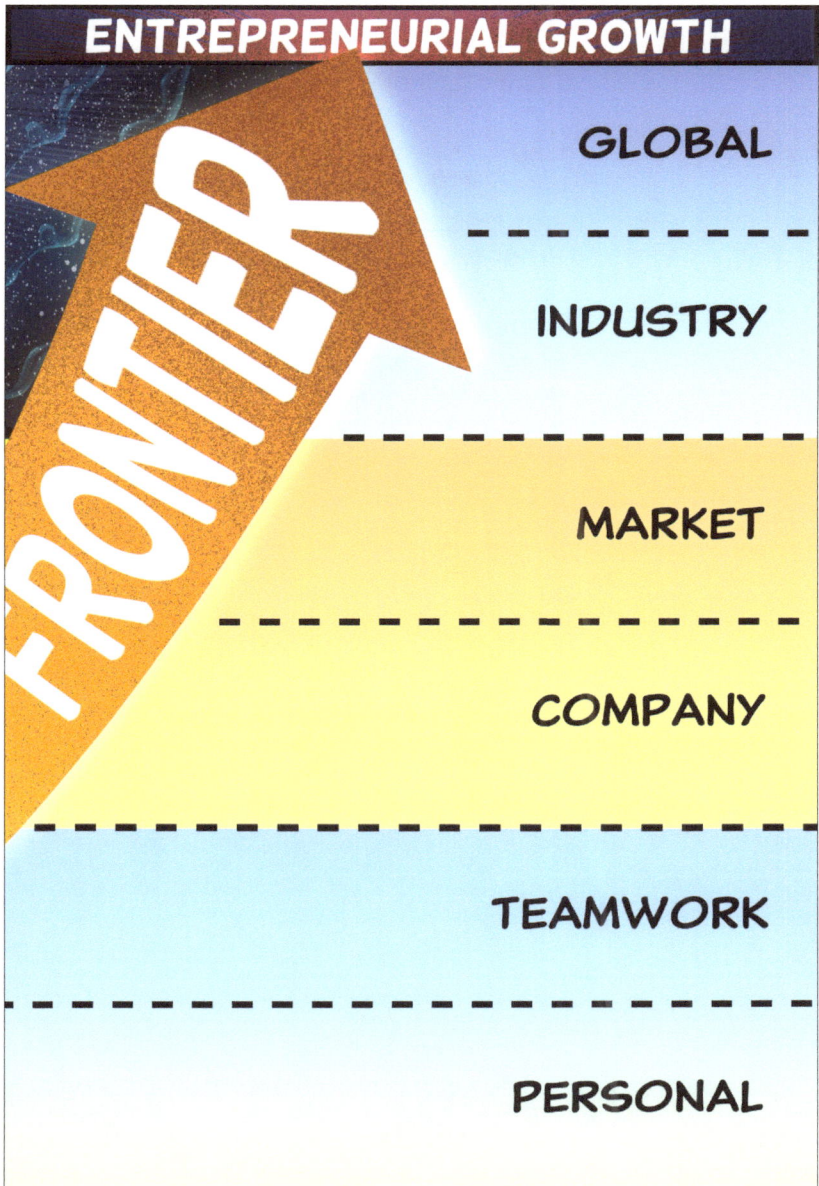

ENTREPRENEURIAL GROWTH

FRONTIER

GLOBAL

INDUSTRY

MARKET

COMPANY

TEAMWORK

PERSONAL

Dan Sullivan

Dan Sullivan is the founder and pres-ident of The Strategic Coach Inc. and creator of The Strategic Coach® Program, which helps accomplished entrepreneurs reach new heights of success and happiness. He is author of over 50 publications, including *The Great Crossover, The 21st Century Agent, Creative Destruction, How The Best Get Better*, and The Ambition Series of quarterly small books. He is co-author of *Who Not How, The Laws of Lifetime Growth*, and *The Advisor Century*.